The Meaning of Life

Other Books by Dean Gualco

What Happened to the American Dream? (1996)

The Meaning of Life

Dean Gualco
Author of What Happened to the
American Dream?

iUniverse, Inc.
New York Lincoln Shanghai

The Meaning of Life

Copyright © 2005 by Dean Gualco

iUniverse books may be ordered through booksellers or by contacting:

iUniverse
2021 Pine Lake Road, Suite 100
Lincoln, NE 68512
www.iuniverse.com
1-800-Authors (1-800-288-4677)

ISBN-13: 978-0-595-35905-9 (pbk)
ISBN-13: 978-0-595-80360-6 (ebk)
ISBN-10: 0-595-35905-1 (pbk)
ISBN-10: 0-595-80360-1 (ebk)

Printed in the United States of America

To my children,
Gunner and Tori,
who have given me a blessed life.

At the end of your life, you should be able to say
that you did the best you could with what you had.
That you fought the good fight.
That you did what was right.
And that, most importantly, in some small way
you made a difference in this world.

Contents

Section 4: Make a Difference. 59

This section further discusses the importance of making a difference in your world. It includes conversations about how to do the best you can with what you have, having the will to act, and always looking for what's next.

Section 5: A Life Lived. 71

This final section covers the importance of being grateful for your life's blessings, endeavoring to live in such a way that you become a hero to others, and making your life an adventurous journey—because life does go by so very quickly.

Introduction

The preeminent question of our time—What is the meaning of life?—has been pondered by great philosophers (including Socrates and Henry David Thoreau) and debated by the most eminent organizations (the world's religions and academic institutions). Undeniably, there are very few people who, particularly as they enter the middle and later stages of their lives, haven't considered what it means to live life: Why am I here? What am I meant to do? What am I meant to be? Have I accomplished anything of value in my life? What is my legacy?

This book arose out of my own search for meaning in my life. This search was prompted, more than anything else, by two realizations:

First, time. I became more conscious that it goes by much too quickly. Life seems to pass by so many people. The precious gift of time is given to each of us without any certainty, without the promise of a tomorrow. Therefore, as the saying goes, never put off until tomorrow what you can do today.

Second, regrets. I became more familiar with people who were entering the closing stages of their lives, who had profound regrets about what little they had accomplished during their time on earth. These people said that if they could do it over again, they would have overcome their jealousies and insecurities, and any other obstacles along their paths, and would have followed their own courses. In doing so, they would have left as "someone of value" in their families and their communities; their time on earth would have been worthwhile; and their lives would have had a purpose.

I became determined to not let regrets happen to me; I was determined to overcome my insecurities, to chart my own path, and to be able to say, when I looked back over my life as it near its end, that I fought the good fight, did what was right, and worked every day to make someone better or something greater.

And if I can do that, my regrets will be fewer and, more importantly, my life will have meaning. I will have mattered. I will have, in some small way, made the world a better place.

Acknowledgments

I would like to extend my gratitude and appreciation to the following people, without whose contributions I would not be the man I am today:

- To "the man above," who has made this all possible.

- To my parents who, throughout my life, have provided a shining example of how to live a decent and honorable life.

- To John Ellis. If you ever wonder what a true friend is, one who possesses honor, unsurpassed loyalty, and genuine goodness, John's the perfect example. You'll never know how much I value our friendship.

- To Keith Williams, the first real friend I ever had. Friends come and go, but there always seems to be one or two you're stuck with for life. Keith is that friend. And to his awesome wife, Sarah, for always treating me as a member of her family.

- To John Solheim, a truly unselfish person who constantly makes me a better person.

- To my Sigma Chi brothers—Phil, Kyle, and Bill—who not only represent memories of yesterday but hopes for tomorrow.

- To Kirk Davis, a genuinely nice guy who reminds me to be positive about life.

- To my alma maters, California State University at Fresno and the University of Southern California, whose teachers pushed me to be the best I could be while not forgetting to give something back along the way.

- Finally, to my children. I hope this book shows you that you can conquer your insecurities, that you can overcome your burdens, that goodness always triumphs over evil, that you must always do what is right, and most importantly, that the good life is possible for those who follow their dreams and help others along the way. That is my dream for you, and it is my life's ambition to help you achieve it.

Section 1:
The Meaning of It All

Use your talents to, in some small way,
make a difference in this world.

THE MEANING OF LIFE

What is the meaning of life? It is a central question that has perplexed men for centuries and yet, in many respects, there still isn't a solid understanding of life and its meaning to the human race.

Viktor Frankl wrote, "To find deeper meaning, according to someone's opinion, one must be able to transcend the narrow confines of a self-centered existence and believe that one will make a significant contribution to life." Author Leo Rosten said, "Nothing is more rewarding than the effort a man makes to matter—to count, to stand for something, to have it make some difference that he lived at all." In some way, then, a sense of meaninglessness arises when an individual, in looking back over his life, feels that he has not accomplished anything of value—there are no monuments or testaments to mountains climbed or deeds worthy of great men.

This leads to my definition of life. In many ways, it is quite simple: Using your talents to, in some small way, make a difference in this world. Whether it is by working with the environment, our educational system, those with physical or mental challenges, or those in the dawn or twilight of their lives, you can achieve meaning in your life by working toward and leaving behind something of value for future generations. It matters little whether your aspiration or dream was realized: we will never have global peace, or feed the world's hungry, or avoid catastrophic diseases or illnesses. What matters is that you tried, that you worked to make the world a better place. **What matters is that, when you look back over your life, you can say that you fought the good fight, that you did what was right, and that you made a difference in this world.**

If you can say that as you enter the later stages of your life, my friend, you will have earned the right to say that your life had true meaning, that you did, in some way, make a difference.

"A man is not finished when he is defeated.
He is finished when he quits."

Richard Nixon

BETTER THE WORLD

A person's value in life is determined less by the car he drives, the house he lives in, the job he has, or the amount of money he has in his bank account; it is determined more by what he has done with what he has. More importantly, a person's life is often valued by what he has left behind or, to be more accurate, how he made the world a better place.

Any discussion on how to better the world starts and ends with education and its value to society. I believe that those who do not know what is good cannot do what is good; those who know what is good will instinctively do what is good. And most importantly, it is education that provides this knowledge. In other words, education provides the foundation upon which one learns what is good, and then—in most cases—also leads him to do what is good. Formal educational settings aren't the only source of such knowledge, however. One can also find it by doing a concentrated study of those people and circumstances that have made the world a better place to live, for example, by reading books that detail how seemingly average people overcame Herculean odds to achieve remarkable goals.

As individuals become better, so will society. Consider any society in history that was the greatest of their day: Rome, Egypt, China, Spain, Britain, and the United States. During their respective periods of greatness, their people had the highest educational levels possible. They directed their energies toward building empires that were the envy of the day. And is the role of education today the same? Most certainly. Its goal is to provide people with knowledge about how to think, with the hope that they will then use those thinking skills to do the right thing, which, for right now, is only for themselves but, later, will also help future generations. To be sure, though, not everyone who is educated does the right thing. There have been extremely educated (and intelligent) people in our history that were also morally deficient. They are the exception, and certainly not the rule.

Charles Jones said, "You are the same person today as you will be in five years, except for two things: the people you associate with and the books you read." Education introduces you to interesting people and great literature, which help you become a great person. And when you become great, you will certainly dedicate any additional knowledge, skills, and abilities you continue to acquire to noble goals. You will, by your very behavior and actions, make the world a better place to inhabit, not only for yourself but also for future generations.

The crowning glory of man is to leave the world better than he found it. To accomplish this, you must know what is right and do what is right, and never waiver from it.

"If you don't know what you stand for, you'll stand, and fall, for anything."

Unknown

WHAT YOU STAND FOR

One of the great searches in life is for personal character—what we stand for—what we truly believe in. Character is a fundamental statement about what defines our path in life, what we are willing to accept and give, and what typifies our character.

The following epitomizes what I stand for:

Do the best you can with what you have. Each person has certain talents and abilities that are unique. Using your talents to their fullest potential will result in greatness; happiness and contentment will surely follow.

You can only achieve such greatness, however, by mastering your fear of failure, which is a natural consequence of daring mighty things. You must, over any other impediment in life, at least take the chance, no matter the outcome. Two quotes come to mind:

- "Aim high enough and you will always fail." (Unknown)

- "You may be disappointed if you fail, but you're doomed if you do not try." (Beverly Sills)

Be able to say that you did the best with what you had, and greatness will be your legacy.

Never place your self-worth or sense of happiness in someone else's hands. It has been said, "Follow your passion in life, no matter the criticism or adversity encountered." It is appropriate to listen to your friends and family for advice; it is not appropriate to be paralyzed by it.

Often, people's apprehensions and fears become apparent in their discussions with you; their words or actions may be critical or even disparaging. In such instances, remember: if you are a cow and someone calls you a zebra, it does not make you a zebra. You must not allow others to alter your self-worth. Never give in to negativity or jealousy from others. It will cloud your judgment and destroy your confidence, self-respect, and self-esteem.

Remember to listen to your heart; make sure you follow your own path in life no matter where it leads. Life is a journey of excitement and self-fulfillment, regardless of whether you ultimately achieve your goal, because at the end, it is the journey that we remember, not the eventual accomplishment.

Stand up for what is right, even if you stand alone. Doing what is right is often not popular. In fact, if what you do is popular, it is often the wrong thing to do. And what is right? I believe that what is right is that which improves human-ity and makes our world a better place.

Pursuing what is right requires a great deal of self-confidence and a lack of self-interest. These are qualities that are difficult to acquire, but even more difficult to lose once acquired.

Be grateful for what you have, not ungrateful for what you do not have. We must be eternally grateful for the gifts and talents we have been granted or have developed throughout our lives. Remember, very few people have the same talents that you do. This gratefulness and accentuation on the positive is best typ-ified in the following anecdote I once came across: "There once was a little girl who cried because she had no shoes, until she saw a little girl with no feet."

Enjoy your life. It goes by in a blink. True happiness and contentment come from those who make the most of whatever time they have. This is your one and only chance; you can never recapture the time you spent in the past. Spend your time doing what you love with people who are important to you.

In some small way, leave the world a better place than you found it. Vic-tor Frankl once wrote, "To find meaning in life one has to transcend the narrow confines of a self-centered existence and believe one can truly make a difference." In most cases, making a difference involves working with those who are less for-tunate, with the environment, or with causes that make this world a better place to inhabit not necessarily for our generation but for future generations. This thought is best typified in the following quote by William Penn:

"I expect to pass through life but once. If, therefore, there be any kindness I can show, or any good thing I can do for any fellow being, let me do it now and not defer or neglect it, as I shall not pass this way again."

This concept comes from the realizations that we should be grateful for what we have, that life goes by so quickly, that we must do what is right, that we must do the best with what we have, that we determine our own value and worth, and that we must leave the world a better place than when we found it. These are the realizations that frame our future. It is most important to realize that through helping others we help ourselves and make our world more pleasant—a place that offers happiness, contentment, and a genuine sense of peace.

Section 2:
The Great Challenges

THE CHALLENGES OF LIFE

In order to lead a meaningful life—one in which you can achieve happiness and peace—you must work to overcome the challenges and obstacles that are an inherent part of every life. Some must overcome mental and physical disabilities, others family problems, and still others financial or cultural issues.

There are certain challenges that, if not addressed, lead to a life of profound difficulty. These challenges, what I call the "Challenges of Life," are so great that they pervade your character, impacting nearly every action and decision you make. Life doesn't need to be that way. You can overcome these challenges with great thought and deliberation toward making yourself a better person, one who chooses the right goal for the right reason.

The four Challenges of Life are as follows:

- **Insecurity.** Insecurity is the most damaging challenge. An insecure person lacks a basic sense of worth. Insecurity manifests itself as difficulty in forming and maintaining real relationships, in putting any degree of trust in people, or in having any sense of peace. Insecurities thwart your ability to take pride in your accomplishments, thus robbing you of true happiness.

- **Self-interest.** Sadly, so many people think of themselves before they think of others. An attitude of self-interest, coupled with a challenging interpretation of morals and ethics, can lead people to do things that benefit themselves in the short run, but harm so many others in the long term. It is ultimately a destructive attitude.

- **Ego.** A person's inability to control his ego leads him to believe that he is both smarter and worth more than others. For people in leadership and decision-making roles, ego prevents them from appreciating the importance of others, and leads them to believe that they can never stumble or make a mistake (therefore, they tend to be inflexible). A person must control his ego to truly be able to see and believe the worth in others.

- **Lack of Self-esteem.** Those who lack a genuine sense of "self" cannot think for themselves or follow their own life path. This lack of self-esteem complicates their leadership and decision-making abilities and, ultimately, prevents them from pursuing options or alternatives that are in the best interest of themselves and their organization. This mainly arises from their fear of failure, which is the natural result of daring mighty things (though other factors influence your fear of failure as well, including childhood upbringing and personality). People must believe they can make a genuine contribution to this world, and that they possess the needed skills and abilities to do so, before they can appreciate the unique talents in us all.

Everyone has something they wish they didn't have. The real challenge is to do something with what you do have.

YOUR LOT IN LIFE

At some point in your life you may encounter a situation that you are not only unprepared for, but that will profoundly alter the direction of your life. It may be the birth of a child with a serious medical disability, financial ruin resulting from the unexpected loss of a job, or perhaps a random act of violence done against you or someone you love. These events are so traumatic and destabilizing that they put you into a state of shock and disbelief that pervades most of your thoughts and actions for the foreseeable future.

For the most part, it is difficult to find any rhyme or reason as to why these events occurred or why they occurred to you. You are at the wrong place at the wrong time and have an automobile accident. You invest in a company a week before they are rocked by accounting irregularities. A routine medical examination is followed by news that you have a serious health crisis. Upon the realization that your life will never be the same, your first thought is, "Why me?" You have followed the rules of life, donated your time and money to worthy causes, and lived a decent and honorable life. Why did this misfortune not happen to those who were selfish, reckless, or added very little to the betterment of mankind? That is one of those unanswerable questions in life; no one on earth knows why you were chosen, but chosen you were.

It becomes your "lot in life." It is the challenge of your life, the burden you must carry. And while it may seem unfair that you must confront that challenge or assume that burden, recognize that everyone has an equal challenge or burden in life. You may not know others' challenges or burdens from what you see of them: it may be their health, which you cannot see, or their lack of family and friends, which you would not know about if they did not share it with you. The key is that everyone has something they wish they did not have. Those who lead a life of great joy and happiness, however, are those who learn to confront their challenges and bear their burdens and do the best with what they have, while recognizing that someone else surely has it worse.

And so the central question becomes: What are you going to do with your lot in life? Are you going to deny its existence or bemoan your fate, or are you going to accept the burden that you must carry and make the best of what you have? Long ago, I chose to accept my lot in life, to recognize how lucky I am—by realizing that so many others have it so much worse—and to do the best I can with what I have. It is, I think, the best way to live a life of meaning.

Always have options in life, for they allow you to get out of situations that compromise your pride, integrity, or sense of self-worth.

GET OUT

At some point in your life—if you have not already—you may find yourself in a situation that you never expected. It may be a situation with a physically or mentally abusive spouse, with disingenuous or dishonest friends, or with a supervisor who is totally devoid of integrity and compassion. Whatever the situation, you are confronted with three choices: try to make it better, learn to live with it, or get out.

Try to make it better. At least initially, we believe the situation can get better—that through conversation with the antagonist, he will see the error of his ways and "repent." However, this belief assumes that all people are reasonable and rational, which we know is not the case; if it is morning, there will be someone who argues that it is evening. While this may be an exaggeration, it reinforces the point that some people are simply not reasonable and, therefore, you have little chance of making things better with them.

Learn to live with it. This is the most destructive choice because you accommodate and compromise your life to allow others to continue their abusive or inconsiderate behavior toward you. If the issue or situation is important to you, you will find that you really cannot "learn to live with it" because it violates your sense of conduct and dignity. If you do try to live with it, you will not live your life but someone else's, which affects your self-esteem and confidence—a circumstance that will then affect your overall sense of worth. The results are indeed catastrophic, affecting your happiness and sense of peace.

Get out. If the issue is important to you—one that is paramount to your sense of righteousness and human dignity—you really have only one choice: *get out*. Leave the situation and move on to a better, though different, life. Some will say that's easier said than done. You may have children to care for and thus cannot leave an abusive relationship; or you may need the income and thus cannot leave a job with a destructive supervisor; or you do not have any other friends and thus need the few you have.

No matter the justification offered, you can get out of nearly every situation. What is critical, though, is that you have options. Money in the bank (or access to money) gives you the option to leave a relationship or a bad job. Formal education provides the option to pursue another job or another career. A group of good friends or a strong social circle gives you the option to leave a dishonest friend. Self-esteem, self-confidence, and self-worth give you the option to confront those who abuse you and the ability to be more accepting of the consequences.

In a nutshell: Remember that you cannot always make things better. Some people are insecure, mean-spirited, or self-interested, so there is little hope to resolve the situation. If you can live with it, be sure that the circumstance does not change your basic disposition—who you are and where you want your moral and ethical life to go. And if you cannot change or live with the situation, for goodness' sake, *get out*. While the future may be less certain than the present, what you do know is that you can get out because you have options in life: you have family, friends, education, talents, abilities, and a belief in your future. Such options give you a sense of confidence. Though there may be challenges along your journey, it will be your life, and your path, that you take. Never accept that which is unjust. Never accept that which is not right. Know that it can get better.

Though there may be some truth to the adage that the grass isn't always greener on the other side, it does not mean that the "shade of green" isn't better than what you now have. It is a difficult choice, to be sure, but it is a choice that makes the difference between a life lived and a life followed. Be sure, when you come to the end of your life, that you can say you got there on the right path.

"Others may hate you, but they don't win unless you hate them back, and then you destroy yourself."

Richard Nixon

THEY MUST LIVE THAT LIFE

Becoming a good person—one who thinks well of others and works to better the lives of those around him—is a challenge in today's world. Negativity can be pervasive, and our culture tends to emphasize traits of resentfulness and jealousy rather than helpfulness and decency. We live in a world where short-term friends, marriages, and jobs are more often the rule rather than the exception, a world where we see that those who do wrong get ahead, while those who do right stay behind.

It is a world where selfish employees—who have ethical standards that are suspect at best—receive the higher merit increase or promotion; where duplicity is rewarded and honesty is often mocked; where management is more interested in getting the sale rather than knowing what you had to say or do to get it. And what of those who do get the sale? They are showcased as examples of what is good and right in the company. They are models of success, examples to emulate.

Most troubling are those who take credit for someone else's efforts, who disseminate blame on those who are not at fault, and who malign and slander others with false statements behind their backs—robbing them of the opportunity to defend themselves. When you are the victim of such deception, you often don't know that it's happening until it is too late, when your personal integrity, professional reputation, and character already have been irrevocably maligned. In these cases, you become damaged not through your own actions—a circumstance that you could more readily accept—but through the misguided and malicious ambitions of others.

This is a perilous situation; but what should you do? First, be aware. Think well of others and work to better your fellow man, but be careful not to let your own basic decency and goodness preclude you from assessing the intentions and motivations of others.

Secondly, and more importantly, never forget that the perpetrators must live that life. Those who wallow in lies and deceit face a life of disappointment and degradation—and their friends and those they seek comfort in as they progress through life will be of the same character. Their life will be consumed with negativity and ill will. And though they may have the material possessions of one who appears to be a success, a genuine sense of sadness will pervade their inner being and consume their life. The life they choose, the life they lead, will eventually become a life of profound unhappiness. Why? Because they haven't lived an admirable life or possessed a respectable character. They have not mattered.

In the end, it may be a challenge not to join them on the journey, even though they may obtain certain material possessions by doing wrong that you would not earn by doing right. But don't worry: the qualities you must have to do wrong are not noble, nor are they worthy. Those qualities pervade a life, and it becomes a life of deceit. Eventually, the price will be paid; let those at the other end of the "goodness spectrum" be the ones to pay it.

Not every battle needs to be fought, nor every hill climbed to the top.

IS IT A HILL?

When should you get involved? When should you interject yourself into a situation that does not directly affect you, yet occupies your interest or concern? Sadly, all too often we become embroiled in situations that do not require our involvement, our advice, or our effort. Whether it comes from your ego ("I can fix it"), your self-interest ("I have to make sure this side wins"), or your need to meddle, your concern is sometimes unwarranted and, in many instances, ends in a personal tragedy of epic proportions.

Of course, there are occasions when your involvement serves a noble purpose. Whether it is an instance of injustice against someone less fortunate, or of dishonesty or duplicity against someone without the will or ability to defend themselves, there are times when you should become involved; though it does not directly affect your person, your basic sense of decency and justice demands that you do it. And you should, for it is the right thing to do.

For many, the challenge is determining when and when not to get involved. When faced with this challenge, ask yourself: Is this situation a hill for me? Is it worth my time and effort to fight the battle? Am I involved for the right reasons? Is it worth any repercussions I may (or, quite frankly, will) confront as a result of my involvement, such as the expenditure of my goodwill or damage to my good name? Is it worth the stress, both physically and mentally, that will surely follow if the issue is of any great substance? If you can answer all of the above questions with a resounding yes, then you *must* get involved. You must get involved because it is the right issue, at the right time, and for the right reasons. To not do so would be unconscionable.

Most interestingly is that the more you ask yourself whether you should climb the hill, the more you realize that you do not need to climb so many, except those that become momentous, because they are central to your values and character. In those instances—although you may be doubtful of the outcome and certain of the struggle—the cause is worthy of your interest and effort. In those cases, you must climb.

Every failure offers a lesson, every success a lesson learned.

LEARN THE LESSON

If you want to accomplish great things in life—if you want to dare mighty things regardless of the consequences—you will, at some point, fail. These failures or mistakes do not always result from a lack of effort, planning, talent, or ability, but instead come from circumstances over which you have little control (for example, global economic collapses or an illness), or from situations caused simply by bad timing or bad luck. Whatever the reason, the result is the same: a failure that belies the considerable time and valiant effort you invested.

Some failures are spectacular. Howard Hughes tried to fly the "Spruce Goose," but it rose for only a minute or so before landing. New Coke was designed to replace classic Coke, but the company quickly reversed its course after a hailstorm of criticism. Or, on a personal level, you misjudged the actions or intentions of a family member, friend, or colleague, who then deceived your trust. Despite your good intentions, expert research and design, and passionate support, a result not of your liking or choosing presented itself.

Failure is disappointing, even devastating to some, but the unintended consequences of failure offer an opportunity: to learn a lesson. For Howard Hughes, the lesson was that technology was not yet able to support his vision. For Coke, the lesson was that its flagship brand could never be altered, and that it would have to develop a different product rather than retooling the original. For you, when you are deceived or devastated, the lesson is to recognize certain traits or characteristics in others that give you a greater insight into who they are and what their interest in you is. The question is: will you learn the lesson?

For some, if not many, their ego and instinctive desire to look for others to blame precludes them from fully understanding, or appreciating, any lesson that's been offered. Statements such as "I don't make those kind of mistakes," or "If Bill would have done what I told him…" are illustrative of those who are destined to repeat the mistakes and failures of their past. They evade the honest assessment of why things occurred as they did. As such, they never realize—nor can they possibly work toward—ensuring that what occurred in the past doesn't happen again (or ensuring that what should have occurred will happen the next time around).

So never hesitate to take that chance; never waiver in your determination to realize your potential. But be prepared to learn the lesson. When failure presents itself or mistakes arise, be willing to face the hard realities of why events happened as they did. Only then can you lessen the chances of failing and encountering defeat in that area again; only then, can you ensure that you will continue on your journey. For only when you learn the lesson can you defeat failure; and only when you overcome failure can you realize your life's ambitions.

"Live your life in such a way that even the undertaker is sorry to see you go."

Mark Twain

DO THE BEST WITH WHAT YOU HAVE

There are many challenges in life, which often come in the form of money, time, health, or knowledge. I am convinced that everyone in this life is given certain advantages (which I call talents) and disadvantages (which I call obstacles). In effect, every person you meet has certain advantages that they are quite proud of—some you can see (looks, money, health), and some you cannot see (intelligence, courage, etc.) Every person also has disadvantages, which we do not often see, because they have worked a lifetime to conceal them from others (insecurities, lack of self-confidence, physical attributes, etc.)

No matter what advantages you have received (talents) or developed throughout your lifetime (skills, knowledge, and abilities), remember these two important thoughts:

- First, take a chance. Beverly Sills says, "Dreams will not keep; something must be done about them." So dream the noble dream, and then use those advantages that you have developed and refined to reach it. Pursuing objectives and results that no one else has achieved takes great courage, and you will surely encounter resistance. Do not pay heed to such resistance. Someone once said, "Pay no attention to what the critics say; no statue has ever been erected to a critic."

- Second, do the best with what you have and then hope for good fortune. You do not necessarily achieve success in your life by reaching your goals, but by taking the journey. Work hard and remain dedicated to your cause, but remember that everyone needs a little luck and good fortune to help the process along.

President Ulysses S. Grant once said, "There are but few important events in the affairs of man brought about by their own choosing." What he meant was you can try as hard as you can to devote yourself to obtaining your goals, but sometimes circumstances outside your control arise that alter your path. This, of course, does not diminish your journey or your accomplishment.

You may not achieve many of your dreams, and if you do, maybe you did not dream high enough. As was once said, "Aim high enough and you will always fail." (Unknown)

If you can do this, if you can do the best with what you have, it will become the journey of your life, and you will leave something behind that you and your family can be proud of.

Section 3:
A Better Person

It is not the mistakes in life that define your character—it is what you do once the mistake has been made.

TAKING RESPONSIBILITY

"It is not my fault." "If you hadn't done that, I wouldn't have done this." "My parents weren't around when I was young; they were always working." "My boss only cares about making money and treats his employees as numbers." How often have we heard those statements? We live in the era I affectionately call the "It Is Not My Fault for My Lot in Life Era." Others simply call it the "Lack of Personal Responsibility Era." Either name works, and both names describe a mentality that is destructive to an individual's development and society's general well-being.

No one is born and raised without burdens or hurdles. Some are born in economically distressed households, some with cancer; some live in a one-parent household, some in an emotionally abusive household; some have to attend schools that are less than adequate. Then, every person acquires additional burdens or hurdles as his life progresses, for example, an unfortunate marriage, an inability to have children, a less-than-desirable job or profession, or a lack of true friendship and companionship.

> *Not everyone has it all.* I have yet to meet an individual who has everything life has to offer, such as fame, fortune, looks, a great family, and friends that are the envy of everyone. In reality, that person does not exist. I used to think John F. Kennedy Jr. had it all, until I realized he lacked the advantage of having a father for most of his life, as well as time on this earth (he died in his thirties). Who would want to change places with him?

- *Do something about your situation in life.* If you find yourself in a situation that is uncomfortable, untenable, or disheartening, for goodness's sake do something about it. In such situations, you are left with two choices: blame someone else for your fate or *do something about it.* Many people tend to blame others, which is destructive to the others as well as to themselves. Blame creates and perpetuates negativity and, most importantly, does nothing to address any disadvantageous life circumstances.

Do something! Attaining a happy life—a life of pure contentment and peace—requires you to take responsibility for that disadvantage that was either given to you (for example, a physical condition, or mental challenges) or that you acquired (for example, poor financial or marital choices you may have made). Having a happy life requires you to recognize that everyone has something to overcome, and those who do overcome reach their potential and enjoy a fruitful and enviable life.

Taking responsibility is not easy. It is so much easier to blame someone else, but then your life does not change. Be great enough to say, "I did not ask for this burden," or "I created this burden, but I am going to overcome it. I will use my talents, family, friends, and the other advantages I have been given to make my life just a little bit better." Fight the good fight and, even if you do not fully reach your destination, know that you have done the best with what you have been given and have developed. You cannot ask for anything more than that.

Taking responsibility for the past and future is the mark of a mature, well-adjusted, and confident person. This maturity comes by realizing that anything is possible, that you can make anything better, and that you can overcome any situation, if only you devote your mind and heart to the endeavor. Years ago I read a story about ten people who were asked to write on a piece of paper the one trait, characteristic, or life circumstance that they had experienced and wish they had not. Some wrote "cancer," "a severe financial strain," and another "a life free from physical harm from my husband." Then they were asked to put all of those pieces of paper in the middle of the group. The group was told: "We can make your particular burden or circumstance go away, but there is a catch. You must then assume someone else's burden or circumstance. You must choose one from the pile."

When everyone chose a circumstance from the pile, they realized their burden was not as difficult as others in the room. They would have rather had their own challenge. Why? Because they had learned how to accommodate their own burdens in life. They also realized that in comparison to everyone else there, they did not have it so bad.

Everyone has some obstacle or impediment. Those who succeed in life have learned either to live with that impediment or to overcome its effects. Those who do not learn are destined for a life of missed opportunities and broken dreams.

Years ago, a friend said to me, "Figure out what you want someone to say at your funeral and live your life backwards." Live life so that your family and friends can say at your funeral, "Some may have thought he had a tough life, and yes, he did have obstacles. But he persevered through the trials and tribulations, he fought the good fight, and he overcame with courage and tenacity whatever flew his way; now rests a person who led a great life and is surrounded by great people. We are fortunate to have known someone who made the world just a little bit better by living."

If you can pass through the unkind words and thoughts you have about others, you can repass through the unkind words and thoughts that are said about you.

PASS AND REPASS

When my grandmother was a young mother, her husband left her for another woman. Though she had every reason to be resentful, she told herself to "pass and repass."

When my mother was a young child, Grandma not only raised her without a father who was around every day, but without one who financially supported her at all—no alimony, no child support. This was many years ago when few opportunities were available to women, so my mother and her family relied on welfare to provide the basic necessities of life. More difficult for my mother, though, was the absence of any cards or gifts from her father during her youth and the ridicule from her classmates because she wore shoes that did not match and clothes that did not fit. Though she had every reason to be bitter, she was taught to "pass and repass."

I remember being the poor athlete in my youth and the one typically chosen last for the team. I also recall, less than fondly, being far from popular among my peers. Though this fostered a sense of insecurity during my formative years, my mother constantly encouraged me to "pass and repass."

What does it mean to "pass and repass," and how can doing so bring so much solace and peace to those who encounter, at times, the worst that life has to offer? One who says "pass and repass" means that life is a continual transition from one state or circumstance to another. What happens today will most likely not happen tomorrow. It means that "this too shall pass."

More importantly, however, "pass and repass" is a reminder that you will experience periods of profound anger and loss in this life. Often, these experiences are the result of what is done to you by other people, whether by your family, friends, coworkers, acquaintances, or those you meet just once. You have a choice: you can become bitter and resentful, or you can remember to "pass and repass." Let go of that which is hurtful to you; be reminded that although others have aggrieve you—often by intention and with malice—you will persevere and become an even better person. You have "passed" through the worst that life has to offer and have "repassed" through those who take satisfaction only in tearing others down.

On his last day in office, President Nixon said, "Others may hate you, but they do not win until you hate them back, and then you destroy yourself." Never let others affect your future, your life. Ensure that when those with malicious intentions create obstacles to your happiness, you "pass and repass." You will be able to overcome any difficulty with courage and with the hope that those who inflict such damage on others find, at some point in their lives, the peace that comes with doing the best and thinking the best of those you encounter in your life. Only then can you think well of yourself and be able to "pass and repass" through the best and worst that life has to offer.

"Pay no attention to what the critics say;
no statue has ever been erected to a critic."

Jean Sibelius

WHO CARES WHAT OTHERS THINK?

When you attempt to do great things in life, you often encounter resistance. This resistance often assumes the form of disparaging, degrading, and demeaning remarks made to ridicule those who take a risk and undertake a challenge in an arena few have dared to enter. There are a variety of reasons for this phenomenon:

- First, people may become uncomfortable when you avoid the common path.

- Second, failure is considered catastrophic in many sectors of our society; others may think you strange or abnormal if you take such a risk.

- Third, others may be jealous of you. Attempting to do great things places you on a different plane than others who lack either the talents or courage to attempt them. People who attempt little commonly feel jealousy or envy in response to those who attempt more.

To a certain extent, you are influenced by what others think and say about you. You care, in some way, about the perception and image that other people have of you. You should, to be sure, care about how you are viewed by others—about your reputation. It should concern you, however, if others' thoughts and opinions paralyze you.

Listen carefully to the advice of others; respect their opinions, and take heart in their care and concern. Chart your own course in life, recognizing that the path of greatness is littered with those who have either tried and failed or never tried at all. Endeavor to never join those ranks. Your journey should characterized by positivity, wonderment, and a genuine sense of peace that your path is noble and just, and when others try to denigrate your cause or ridicule your endeavor, consider the following words of solace and guidance:

- If you are a cow and someone calls you a zebra, it does not make you a zebra. In other words, if you know you are a kind and just person of good character, no one can say or do anything to you to make you feel differently.

- Remember Nixon's words: "Others may hate you, but they do not win until you hate them back, and then you destroy yourself." This statement, made during his presidential resignation speech, is a powerful reminder that there are those who may be vigilant in their opposition to you, but you must never feel the same in return or you will damage your character and alter your perspective on life. You may, in effect, destroy your future.

So do the right thing. Fight the good fight. If you do, you will care little about what others think or say about you, and you will overcome a significant obstacle to leading a noble life: the obstacle of what others think about you. In reality, overcoming it is the only way to live a life of passion and adventure, a life truly worth living.

"The world is made up of kings and pawns, but at the end of the game they go back in the same pine box."

Unknown

KINGS AND PAWNS

Some people, such as presidents and philanthropists, are famous for the contributions they make to our society. Others are famous because they have chosen a path in life that greatly interests our society, such as sports, the arts, or politics—from the Super Bowl—winning quarterback to the Academy Award—winning actor. These few possess fame and fortune, and many consider their lives exciting and important. But therein lies the paradox: we only view their lives; we do not live them. We do not know—and they often try to keep quite hidden—their sorrows and disappointments so similar to our own.

I am convinced that all people are born with a certain advantage in life, such as height, dexterity, or intelligence. They may be born into families of great wealth and social stature, or into ones with great love for each other and their fellow human beings. The central point is that all people are born with something—that *one* thing that makes them lucky. And although that gift may not command great attention or create great wealth, it is unique.

What is most interesting is that each of us has such little control over what our gift is. Would Michael Jordon have been the preeminent basketball player of his generation were it not for his height? John McEnroe is often called the most talented tennis player to ever play the game, mainly due to his outstanding hand-eye coordination and tremendous reflexes. Josh Groban and Celine Dion have stunning voices, a talent few others have.George W. Bush was aided considerably in his first election as governor of Texas by his family's political connections and access to significant financial resources. We often applaud the successes of such people and follow in awe their accomplishments.

This brings us to an interesting paradox: why should a person feel superior to any other person based on the fruits of his talent or the gift that he had no hand in choosing? Although society may place a greater sense of worth on those born into a certain family or with certain physical attributes, the holder of the gift has little right to believe he is better than anyone else. He has little right to believe he earned it or that it is part of his destiny. He does have a right to be grateful for that which is given to him, and to then do something with it—something that shows that he made the most of what he got.

The mark of a great person is applauding, without envy or jealously, those whose gifts bring fame or fortune. And people with such gifts have a profound responsibility to remain humble—humble in the realization that although they have expended great effort in their endeavor, so much of what they achieved was due to what they were given rather than to what they earned.

Never forget that we all have been born with something unique in this world. We all have something that someone else will spend his life trying to obtain, to no avail. That something is our gift. It is what makes us so lucky in this world. It is what makes us all kings.

You can never be better than someone else, only better than you were yesterday.

Never place your self-worth in someone or something, for disillusionment and disappointment will surely be the hallmarks of your life.

ARTIFACTS AND ACCOLADES

It seems that for some people the richness of life lies in their possessions. For some, it is being named the "best" in this contest or the "greatest" in that event. For others it is having the mansion on the hill or the prestigious title at a renowned organization. Whatever the accolade, whatever the artifact, their possession drives some to forsake all else with the hope that the possession will, in some way, convey a sense of accomplishment, importance, and value to their lives.

And does it? Does money convey a sense of accomplishment for some, or winning the game a sense of importance for others? Will you have more friends or relationships because you have become a "somebody" (or, more accurately, a "something")? For a brief, shining moment, it may. The Super Bowl and the Academy Awards are among the most watched television events of the year. Those who win encounter fame and fortune, and many people want to join their circle and share the excitement and interest that has befallen them. But does such good fortune last? More importantly, does it impart a sense of inner peace?

Therein lies the first irony of accolades and artifacts: they are so fleeting. Not many could name the Heisman Trophy winner of 1997 or the men's Wimbledon champion in 2001, or even the president of the United States in 1920. These are singular achievements and appointments that recognize one individual during one historical moment.

Second, that which has been achieved can so easily be lost. Though you may have won the World Series this year, you may not next year. Though you may realize your life's ambition to become president of a specific organization, it may be lost next year if that company experiences an accounting scandal or a product defect. Thus, attributing your sense of accomplishment to what you have rather than who you are will doubtless lead to a life of disappointment and disillusionment.

And why do some seek a life dedicated to the pursuit and attainment of accolades and artifacts? For the most part, I believe, out of insecurity, the belief that your worth in life is determined by that which you possess, the belief that to have friends or to be liked you must possess an accolade or artifact. So you spend your life in the pursuit of things, with the hope that those things will translate into a deeper sense of value and worth. Instead, life becomes an endless pursuit in which you never attain enough accolades or artifacts and thus never develop the true sense of security.

Few remember the great men and women of yesterday. Few remember the great deeds made by those with tremendous courage and passion. While unfortunate, it reflects the reality that not only is life fleeting, but so are fame and fortune. Events pass, new champions are crowned, and the victors of yesterday are left with awards that tarnish and memories that fade through time.

And so, never pursue accolades or artifacts simply to have them. Instead, pursue that which uses your talents and convictions toward noble aims. Pursue that which brings you joy and happiness. If you do, your life will be directed toward the right things for the right reasons. You will become the type of person you were meant to be, and that, my friend, would be the greatest accolade or artifact one could hope to possess.

YOUR WORD

The trait that best defines your character, the trait most admired by those you encounter, the trait that tells others who you really are is the extent to which you are able to keep your word. Keeping your word means you are a person of integrity; an honorable person. There can be no greater compliment than for others to say you are an honorable person, that you honor your family, friends, profession, and, most importantly, your word.

Few people intentionally break their word. Most of us want to be considered honorable because image and self-esteem are largely dependent on what others think and say about us. To gain honor, we try to live a life that others respect—to gain admiration and to ensure that our intentions and actions are consistent with society's demands of its citizens. And that starts and ends with keeping our word.

There is much in life, however, that challenges our ability to keep our word. There are circumstances in life, often not of our own choosing, that force us to make a choice. Keeping our word in these circumstances often requires a tremendous sacrifice; that sacrifice could be a job, a considerable amount of money, a valued friendship, or some sacrifice of our physical or emotional pleasure. At times like these, the price to pay for truth may appear to be too high, and we are faced with a dilemma: do we do the right thing and pay the price, or do we do the wrong thing to avoid sacrifice? Unfortunately, we all too often make the wrong choice.

Anytime you break your word, you break your bond with others. Your word is a commitment, a commitment to do or say something important to someone else. When your commitment to another person is broken, so is your relationship with that person. Relationships are built on trust, and, without trust, it is difficult to have faith in others. If you break your word, you entered a path toward loneliness, a path littered with those who fail to keep their word because the sacrifice is too great. It can be a legacy of disappointment and shame, one you avoid if you keep your word.

Be willing to pay the price, overcome any sacrifice, and keep your word. Your reputation is the one aspect of your character most admired by others if intact and the one most difficult to regain if lost. If you can keep your word, others will grant the admiration you seek and recognize you for the honorable life you endeavor to lead.

"After I'm dead I'd rather have people ask why I have no monument than why I have one."

Cato the Elder (234–149 BC)

A DECENT AND HONORABLE PERSON

Decently and *honorably:* no words better describe how you should live your life. I know few people who can be described with those words or who live lives that reflect them. One must endure significant sacrifice and struggle to do so. It is that rare person who does not encounter envy for the way he lives his life, jealousy over the people in his life, or hatred for what he stands for. It is even rarer still for someone to overcome jealousy, envy, and hatred to lead a decent and honorable life.

A decent person is one who is well-mannered, polite, and unfailingly kind. He is respectful of his elders and those less fortunate and treats his family and friends with reverence and endearment. Such a person is someone with whom we are proud to work, play, and be friends. This person is decent because, no matter how he is treated, he treats others with a sense of dignity and compassion uncommon to most people. Decency is a truly virtuous trait.

An honorable person is one who is principled and moral. His intentions are noble, as are his actions. His beliefs, aspirations, and integrity are never compromised, no matter the money, power, or fame offered. Honorable people are good people because they always do the right thing for the right people for the right reason, and we admire and respect them for demonstrating such honor.

Throughout life there will be occasions when we are belittled or defamed, when the only way others can think better of themselves is to put us down. That is to be expected, but the good person, the decent and honorable person, is the one who does not respond in kind. Retaliation and retribution are not part of his repertoire. Through any unkind work or deceitful conduct, the decent and honorable person is the one who lives his life according to a noble standard and refuses to compromise when confronted with those at the opposite end of the moral spectrum.

Live a life in which you are introduced as a decent and honorable person, one in which others refer to you as a decent and honorable person. When your life has ended, let it be said, "Here lies a decent and honorable person." Many aspire to hear such words, yet so few do, and this is truly unfortunate. Only when you lead a decent and honorable life can you attain the peace, security, and genuine sense of contentment that are the hallmarks of the good life. They are the hallmarks of a decent and honorable person.

Section 4:
Make a Difference

You can't do what is right unless you know what is right.

KNOW GOOD, DO GOOD

To be good, one must do good. To do good, one must know what is good, and this is where education plays a formative role.

Gandhi once said, "One cannot be committed to doing good in one area of your life while you are committed to doing bad in another; life is one indivisible whole." In other words, a person cannot better his professional life unless he betters his personal life as well. He cannot make good decisions at home and bad decisions at work.

It is critical that we improve ourselves through education. Why? It has been said that he who would govern others must first govern himself. In other words, if you have any intention of successfully managing people, you must first "know thyself" (as Socrates said) and continually make yourself a better person. Another saying goes, "Hatred against others is inseparable from hatred against oneself." Put more plainly: if you do not like yourself, it is nearly impossible for you to like anyone else.

Martin Luther King Jr. once said that the role of education is to "live well, think wisely, and act sensibly." He did not say that its role is to make more money or earn company promotions. He understood (as we all should) that our role as educators is to improve the person, not only the professional. He understood that time invested in improving oneself cuts down on time wasted in disapproving others. You become better by improving your environment, surrounding yourself with good people, and learning from skilled teachers.

I am absolutely convinced that effective people (and managers) bring a bit of humanity, warmth, and caring to their environment. They create an inviting and supportive place that is conducive to improving their future, but they also encourage and stimulate others to be good and do what is good. People leave positive work environments feeling better about themselves and about the experiences they had.

You cannot help everyone (e.g., some people are not interested in knowing their direction in life, what they stand for, what they should strive for, or how they can better themselves and their environment, etc.), but you should not necessarily be concerned about that. Always look on the positive side; think of those whom you have positively influenced, and your future will comprise invigorating experiences for you and for those with whom you spend your time.

"Dreams will not keep; something has to be done about them."

Beverly Sills

THE WILL TO ACT

Over the course of our lives, we accumulate great knowledge from formal education, professional experience, conversations with colleagues and friends, and family and our cultural heritage. Such knowledge is valuable determining our life's goals, aspirations, and dreams. But there is an unintended consequence of acquiring this knowledge: some people believe that things cannot be accomplished, that the status quo cannot be altered, and that dreams cannot be attained.

Where does this come from? In actuality, it pervades our society. In our youth we are told that we can be anything we want. After high school or college we are told to do something productive and to make a living. In our educations, we study more of what does not work than what does. Negative stories sell newspapers and magazines (e.g., THE FALL OF ___! or ___ AND ___ TO DIVORCE! etc.). When is the last time that you saw a headline that read, THE WEATHER IS GREAT TODAY, or MILLIONS OF AMERICANS HAD A SAFE, PROSPEROUS, AND HAPPY DAY AT WORK TODAY? And in business we are often judged more by our bad decisions and failures than our successes; failures have a more glaring impact on an organization, both politically and financially. Success has many fathers, but who wants to be associated with a failure?

Our culture tends to feed on negative input, on that which reflects poorly on others. We see this when we build people up and then work ardently to bring them down when they cast an unwanted reflection on our own worth. For this reason, many individuals take glee in the demise of Martha Stewart or others who have fallen from grace. People see the viciousness inflicted on others and vow to avoid the same fate. Thus, they become averse to risk and complacent with their fate of mediocrity.

But this does not have to happen. Life must be experienced. It must be lived. You must muster the courage and the will to act. Be thankful for your talents and blessings in life and then act. But then use them in the pursuit of your aspirations and dreams. Do something every day that brings you closer to your life's aspirations. Will there be risk? Absolutely. Will there be failure? Most certainly. But there will neither be cowardice nor a life left unimagined and unfulfilled. Living courageously provides you with great pride in your past and even greater promise for your future. A courageous life is one worth living.

"Do the right thing.
It will gratify some people and astonish the rest."

Mark Twain

DO THE RIGHT THING

You often hear the phrase, "do the right thing," or "stand up for what is right." The key here, of course, is to know what is "right" and how to develop the courage to do "the right thing."

What is "right"? Right is that which advances the public good. In effect, it is what improves the human condition and leaves the world a better place than it was when you found it. Thoughts and actions filtered through that standard clarify one's thinking and lead one to instinctively do the right thing.

We must develop the courage to do the right thing. Most of us know the right thing to do, but we are often presented with obstacles to doing it. This is, in actuality, expected. In his book, *The Art of Happiness,* the Dali Lama said the following:

> Every day we are faced with numerous decisions and choices. And try as we may, we often do not choose the right thing that we know is "good for us." Part of this is related to the fact that the "right choice" is often the difficult one—the one that involves some sacrifice of our pleasure.

Decisions would be easy if there were no cost to them. It is only when there is a cost to our professional or personal desires that we deviate from doing the right thing. We tend to rationalize and justify our decisions so that we do not have to sacrifice any of our pleasures. These rationalizations and justifications are heard in everyday phrases: "I am doing it for my kids," "It will pay off in the long run," or "Everyone else does it." If it were the right thing to do, we would never need to rationalize or justify our actions.

So how do you develop the courage to do the right thing? In a way, it is simple. First ensure that your interests are right (i.e., they better humanity and our society), and then have the self-confidence, pride, and conviction to stand up for what is right, even if you stand alone. Devote your energies to the pursuit of goodness and righteousness. There are so few individuals who do so. I once read that the man who sacrifices his life for justice evidently has motives far superior to most men or a disinterestedness incomprehensible to them. Be that individual who sacrifices for the common good, the person who endeavors to improve those around him and the society in which he lives, and you will be remembered as someone who fought the good fight and did the good deed.

Most importantly, though, you will look back on your life as a journey well-traveled toward aims that were just and noble. You will not only have pride in your accomplishments, but you will receive the admiration of others in your life.

You will have pursued, in effect, what is right. You will have obtained that which makes our world just a little brighter than it was when you found it.

It's not what happened yesterday that controls your destiny; it's what you can do tomorrow.

NEXT

There are few people who do not, at some time in their lives, have regrets. Regrets can be separated into four categories: how you spent your time, how you spent your money, what you accomplished during your life's work, and how you handled your personal relationships. Some may regret not graduating college, spending too much time at work, or not spending enough time with their children. Others may regret how they handled a relationship with a spouse or a friend, how they spent their money, or how they abandoned a passion in life, regardless or in spite of the adversity of criticism encountered.

Little can be done about regret. Although you may wish you had spent more time with your children as they grew up, that time has passed. Although you may wish you had handled your marriage better, that time has passed. Although you may wish that you had devoted more of your efforts bringing yourself joy, that time too has passed, so what comes next?

It should matter little what you regret. You surely wish time could be reversed so you could live through that time again, but it cannot. And while some regrets may afford you the opportunity to make amends—with an apology here or restitution there—others may not. This may cause some individuals to be overwhelmed with unresolvable regrets—a perilous and destructive state.

The key to remaining challenged and optimistic is to focus on what you will do next. Focus today on what you are planning to do tomorrow, the future. When you are laid off from your job, think not on why it happened but on what you can do about it. When personal relationships end catastrophically, think not about what you did, but about how you may better handle your next relationship to ensure a different fate. And when you mishandle your finances and face devastation, think not be about the circumstances of the event but on what you can do today to ensure greater financial security for tomorrow.

Sincerely regret past transgression and inaction, and, when available and appropriate, make sincere and honest amends for your actions. But then move on to what is next: taller mountains to climb and more fascinating buildings to construct. Those instilled with joy in life are those who recognize that life presents many obstacles—some you overcome and others you do not. Some of the obstacles bring out the best in you, and others, the worst. Remain engaged, energetic, and enthusiastic, and realize that life is all about what comes next.

Section 5:
A Life Lived

**Be grateful for what you have,
not ungrateful for what you do not have.**

BE GRATEFUL FOR WHAT YOU HAVE

A fancier car. A bigger house. A better friend. It seems that many people view their importance in life by what they have rather than who they are. While such people may have attained some level of personal and professional success, it is not enough. They want more, not because it necessarily betters society, but because of the misguided belief that having more of everything will better them. Nothing could be farther from the truth.

And so, if you are one of these people, you spend your life trying to get "more." What you have is quickly shadowed by what you do not have. The promotion of today scarcely valuable because the promotion of tomorrow consumes your thoughts. You can't enjoy the new car or home of today because you are thinking of the faster car and bigger home of tomorrow. Your thoughts become consumed by what you do not have, and you mistakenly believe that if you have it, you will become imbued with a genuine sense of peace, security, and happiness.

Peace, security, and happiness, however, are not derived from what you own; they are achieved by doing the best you can with what you have and then profoundly appreciating the bounty in your life. This also includes accepting what did not come your way, and there are very few people in this world who have not, at some point in their lives, wished they had something they did not. And therein lies the lesson.

Accept what you did not get, and appreciate what you did. Value what you have been given, and never long for that which has been taken. Be thankful for those experiences and challenges that have made you the person you are today, even those that may have caused disappointment and regret at some point. Feel fortunate that you at least had a chance in life and that you made the most of it. If you can learn these lessons, you will always be grateful for your life and never envious over the lives of others. And, most importantly, you will experience the peace, security, and happiness many long for but few attain.

Heroes show us what is possible, if we only have the courage to believe if our destiny.

HEROES

Heroes are those whom we admire and emulate. We aspire, to some degree, to be like them or to have what they have, whether fame, fortune, material possessions, physical abilities, mental capabilities, personality, or strength of character. Their lives and accomplishments inspire us. How? Because they made the impossible appear possible and the unbelievable, believable.

Within their particular fields, such as sports, acting, business, or politics, our heroes conquered their doubts and insecurities. They reached the pinnacle of their sport or profession, and they are worthy of our admiration because they used their courage, hope, perseverance, and fortitude to succeed. We hope that by studying their lives we can, to some degree, replicate their paths to success and realize our own dreams and aspirations as well.

My heroes, like so many others, are those who made the most of what they had, never wavered or faltered, and in some small way bettered our world. Those I most admire would include the following people:

- Margaret Thatcher, who believed that through sheer will and fortitude a country can be made great again. She never courted popularity, even when it cost her the prime ministership of Great Britain. She was willing to risk all for the good of her people rather than gain all at their expense.

- Eunice Shriver, who was born into great wealth and privilege as a member of the Kennedy family and who used her position and influential contacts to found the Special Olympics. There are few people with a greater legacy of genuine kindness than Mrs. Shriver.

- Ivan Lendl, the former number one tennis player in the world, who had little talent but a will to be the best he could be. He succeeded by effort; he practiced more than others, played more than others, and worked to best use any advantage he had to win. To others, he showed that it is possible for those with little innate talent to realize their dreams through focus and determination to make the most of what they were given.

- Kurt Warner, the man who rose from working in a supermarket to winning a Super Bowl with the St. Louis Rams. He was waived shortly thereafter because of physical injuries, but he never lost his faith in himself or in those around him and remained a shining example of what is good in sports. He never changed, whether he worked in a supermarket or became a superstar.

Although it is important to have heroes, it is even more important to be a hero. And what do people look for in a hero? They look for someone who does the most with what he has been given; for someone who has overcome great obstacles and persevered through great challenges; for someone who, though scarred by battle, never lost their senses of decency, honor, and goodness, no matter the fame or fortune offered; for someone who, quite simply, fought the good fight; a person who remained true to his character and passion in life.

When looking back over your life, if others can say that you became a hero to them, you will have lived a life in which you have given more than you have taken. You will have shown others that dreams do come true, that greatness can be achieved. You will have left a legacy for others to admire. You would have earned the right, in the end, to be called a hero.

Live a life worthy of tomorrow's heroes.

A true friend is one who endeavors to ease your voyage through life, expecting nothing in return except to share your journey.

A FRIEND

Life, with all of its opportunities and challenges, joys and sorrows, is a fantastic journey. This journey offers the extremes of our world, whether that would be scaling the greatest mountains and experiencing the greatest triumphs or falling into the deepest valleys and experiencing profound disappointment. On this journey, with its trials and tribulations, our will is tested and our fortitude challenged. We never waiver during this journey, not only because of our strength of character, but because we have chosen a select group of individuals to accompany us on these travels. These individuals—we are proud to say—are our friends.

A friend is someone who understands what makes you the type of person you are and who endeavors to help you become the type of person they know you can be. A friend revels in the best things about you and accepts the worst. Friends are there when you need them and, more importantly, when you do not. They know the truth about you, your life, and your ambitions, yet they respect where you are and where you are trying to go. A friend is all of this because, quite simply, a friend cares. A friend cares whether you attain your dreams and ambitions and does all he can to ease your voyage. A friend hopes that any disappointments you face in life are brief and assists you to overcome their effects. A friend cares whether your life's journey is full of great happiness and asks only that, in some small way, he is allowed to share in it.

How important are friends? If you can go through life with true friends equal in number to the fingers of one hand, then you are a fortunate person. You are fortunate because you have friends to share your joy and sorrow, success and failure. Most importantly, you have friends who accept you and encourage you to go where you want. Little else offers so much solace, so much peace, and so much joy as true friends to share the trials and tribulations of life. They make life worth living.

Adventures become the memories of your life.

THE ADVENTURE OF A LIFETIME

Have you ever noticed the genuine wonderment of toddlers as they encounter life and all of its treasures for the first time? An empty box can offer as much joy as an encounter with the Easter Bunny, a set of Tupperware bowls on which to bang, or a colorful flower to smell. No matter the person, the place, or the thing, children want to see and feel and touch; that is how they determine their limitations as they progress through childhood.

As we enter our teenage years and early adulthood, we tend to become more cautious and cognizant of these limitations. Our wonderment wanes, mainly because we fear public ridicule and failure. We temper our ambitions and sense of adventure, and this has catastrophic consequences: we avoid running for student council because we might lose, or we don't try out for the football team because we might not play. Although we are saved the ridicule that might result from daring and failing, we never experience the profound exhilaration of daring and succeeding.

These experiences become the defining moments of our lives because in nearly every adventure we undertake, no matter the destination, we learn about the world and our place in it. You may read about the view of the valley from the mountain, but you cannot experience it until you climb the mountain. You may see a great painting in a book, but you cannot appreciate the subtleties of the brushstrokes unless you see it in a museum. You may watch a NASCAR race on television, but you cannot comprehend the speed and excitement of cars accelerating around a track at 200 miles per hour unless you are there with the other 150,000 spectators. You may see a documentary on poverty or malnourishment, but it does not affect your life until you see for yourself people without food to eat or those struggling with preventable illnesses who simply cannot get the medical treatment they need to survive.

Therein lays the value of living an adventurous life: those who live a life of adventure know what is possible. This is especially important for the young; what they do not experience, they do not realize is possible. They cannot understand who they are or what they can become unless they know what is possible. And it is up to their parents or other loved ones to show them a world of unlimited possibilities—to show them about the arts, sports, and the historical monuments of people and cultures that overcame great obstacles to contribute to this world. While they are still young, they can become exposed to that which is possible, that which they would not have seen had they not embarked on an adventure of discovery and wonderment.

It is to be hoped that the sense of adventure you experience as a child continues throughout the years. You may meet new people, experience different cultures, and visit faraway places. Each new experience alters your perspective and shapes your character. Your constant growth offers the sense of exhilaration and wonderment reminiscent of your childhood. And as your journey through life ends, you may say, "I have experienced everything life has to offer. It is a life that has been lived." Who could ask for more?

"A society grows great when old men plant trees whose shade they know they shall never sit in."

Greek Proverb

IT GOES BY IN A BLINK

Do you remember waiting, as a child, for Christmas to come, thinking it would never arrive? Or do you recall waiting to go on that vacation to Disneyland with the family? You could not *believe* there were still three weeks to go! Our youth is filled with such impatience; we do not have the perspective on time that we develop as we age.

We all eventually confront the profound realization that our lifespan is finite and that we cannot accomplish all that we had wanted. This realization occurs for some of us as we enter our late thirties and early forties, a period of reflection on where we have been, where we are, and where we want to be. It is a time when we might realize that our accomplishments don't measure up to our expectations and that our hopes for ourselves may never be realized. That realization can cause so much disappointment and unhappiness in our lives. We may begin to think that life passes too quickly for us to attain all of our aspirations and dreams, to experience everything that life has to offer. It does not, however, have to be that way.

Some may say that the length of our lives has been predetermined. Others say that lifestyle choices (e.g., smoking, drinking, occupation, etc.) determine the amount of time on Earth. Still others say it is a combination of both. Whichever belief you may have, you must devote your thoughts, energies, and time toward your passions to reach your dreams and aspirations in life and live a life of greatness. If you do, you devote your life to reaching and hopefully obtaining that which makes you who you are. If you are Jeff Gordon, that thing is auto racing. If you are Kenny Chesney, it is singing and performing country music songs. If you are Eunice Shriver, it has been the creation and promotion of Special Olympics. Whatever your passion may be, no matter the diligence or persistence required to achieve your goals, such dreams become reality through time.

I hope you realize that time goes by very quickly. This fundamental realization should awaken your mind and spirit in discovery and devotion to your passion in life. If you come to this realization, the adventure of life will be one of great joy—joy that accompanies a sense of pride and self-fulfillment rarely felt by others. More importantly, you may enjoy contentment, knowing that you did the best with what you had, that you made the most of your talents. At the end of your life you will be able to say that your time went by in a blink…but the time you did have held true meaning for you and others. You mattered.

978-0-595-35905-9
0-595-35905-1

LaVergne, TN USA
19 November 2010

205596LV00001B/6/A